TEA

WESLEYAN POETRY

t e a

BY D. A. POWELL

Wesleyan University Press

Published by University Press of New England · Hanover and London

Wesleyan University Press

Published by University Press of New England, Hanover, NH 03755

Printed in the United States of America

5 4 3 2 1

CIP data appear at the end of the book

For

Scott Gregory Gulvas, for whom I wrote,

and in loving memory

of the many beautiful young men

who have disappeared from my life due to AIDS

CONTENTS

vii

viii

X

This is not a book about AIDS. I offer this at the outset, because I know that in the short-hand way in which books are discussed, catalogued, reviewed, marketed, introduced, AIDS will inevitably be touted as one of the cries of the book's occasion. I do not deny this disease its impact. But I deny its dominion.

I began *Tea* as a chronicle of a relationship. Having not written for a year following the relationship's terminus, I was compelled to begin writing again, and I took my failed relationship as subject. Because I was unable to contain the first lines I wrote, I turned my notebook sideways, pushing into what would traditionally be the margins of the page. These lines, with their peculiar leaps and awkward silences, became the strangely apt vessel into which I could pour my thoughts. I took fragments and made new statements from them, just as I wished to reshape my life from its incomplete bits.

For every thought I had of Scott in writing the first poems, I had as many thoughts of other loves—friends, lovers, "tricks"—who had passed through my life. And so I wrote of them also, reenacting the serial polygamy that had characterized my life. I do not mean for this condition to signify anyone's experience but my own: I had moved through the world a sexual libertine, unfaithful even in the way I conflated the touch of one lover with thoughts about another.

As memory required me to revisit the deaths of many of these men, I realized that I ran the danger of writing a collection in which death was a consequence of my "lifestyle." (I use quotes here, because I do not really understand the difference between a life and a lifestyle, aside from the fingerpointing. I am nevertheless happy to be accused of style.) Some who read or who do not read this book will hold that opinion. But the truth was—is—that my life is a consequence of those deaths. My relationship with Scott was in part a failure of our understanding of the times. Our fear of knowing our own HIV status was one of the powerful forces that held us together and drove us apart: we saw each other alternately as the possibility of salvation and as the possible instrument of destruction. Because of this, we simultaneously loved and hated each other with a kind of emotional violence.

While I was writing these poems, a well-known poet, who is also queer, cautioned me against "using AIDS as a metaphor for a consumptive relationship." I do not understand "metaphor." I have the sort of mind that lumps together odd events, that enjoys the simultaneity of experience. My parents divorced during the Watergate hearings. The backlash against disco coincided with the Reagan administration. I was hospitalized for a nearly fatal accident while my friend Andy was dying, the first of many I would lose to AIDS. If two objects occupy the same space, is one a metaphor for the other? If so, then life is the cause of death; love, the root of unhappiness.

Yet there is a way in which AIDS moves through the text, just as other forces, events and characters move through it. Because I based these poems on my own experience, I had to uncover the subject that drove the writing; and so I had to walk down many corridors in order to find what was at center. Along the way, I had to write about failed love, destitution, prostitution, disease, homelessness, and a myriad other subjects in order to discover that the true hero of the poems is survival. This is how I came to put the elegies at the front of the book. I rise out of ashes. To survive is an astonishing gift. The price of that gift is memory.

*   *   *

The title of the book may puzzle some. Before I wrote *Tea* I had written a collection entitled *Lunch*. *Tea* seemed to be the next logical step. I chose tea as a central figure not only for this reason, but also because it has such wonderful resonance for me. "Tea" was a term from pre-Stonewall days that is still a part of the queer argot. Originally, when queers still referred to ourselves as "queens," "having tea" was a natural extension of one's royal masquerade. However, "tea" the beverage was not necessarily involved in "having tea." Instead, "tea" was a session of gossip exchange. If one was invited to "tea," this usually meant that one was going to be privy to some scandalous information.

 A public area in which men gathered for sex (and gossip too) was hence a "tea room." And the last trip to the bars before the weekend ended—on Sunday afternoons—became the "tea dance." *Tea*. A wonderfully glamorous word to adorn rather unglamorous rituals.

With all of these coded meanings, I suppose one might be tempted to read the title as a furtive gesture. I did not intend to be furtive. Rather, I wished to bring into the language of the poems all of the kinds of speech that I have heard around me—tall speech and short speech, the proper and the vernacular. I honor my dead in the attempt to recapture their voices.

*   *   *

Despite any hardship, I see what a blessing my life has been. I have written this book for the men who did not live to write their own stories: David Damon, Ricky Encinas, Michael Montero, Fidel Bady, Daehn Lebhardt, Lewis Friedman, Victor Martinez, Nick Wilson, Ken Penny, Andy Moore, Jeff Mahoney, Jon Burnett, Ernie Lopes, Sylvester James, Gary Deal: a list that once begun has resisted closure. This is not about being queer and dying. It is about being human and living.

—D. A. Powell, 1997

ACKNOWLEDGMENTS

First, let me gratefully acknowledge the love and support of Barbara Lesch-McCaffry, J. J. Wilson and David Bromige, without whom I never would have stayed in school.

Many talented poets provided advice and suggestions for the manuscript. Especially valuable to me have been the words of James Galvin, Marvin Bell, Robert Hass, Carol Ciavonne, Samuel Witt, Brian Cassidy, Tom Thompson, Valerie Savior, Mary Szybist, Rachel Zucker, John Casteen, Kevin Killian, John Beer, Timothy Liu, Jane Mead, Julia Ward, Scott Coffel, Mary Wang, Katherine Swiggart, Alec Dinwoodie and, most especially, Jorie Graham, whose faith in my project kept me going. I give special thanks to Brenda Hillman, who sent the manuscript to Wesleyan.

Portions of the text first appeared in *Colorado Review, Boston Review, Mirage #4 [Period]ical, Eunuch, Antenym, Phoebe, Boomerang, Volt, Denver Quarterly,* and *Coe Review.* My thanks to those editors as well.

—D. A. Powell

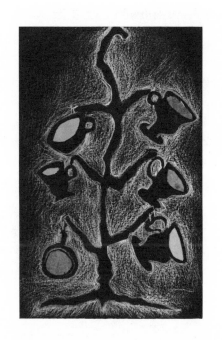

t e a   l e a v e s

"Such are the final, unenviable forms that survival assumes."

—Marcel Proust, *The Past Recaptured*

[to end and to open with a field: andy buried under a hunter's moon. deer born of headlights]

to end and to open with a field: andy buried under a hunter's moon.   deer born of headlights

I had meant to be first among us dead.   swerve toward atonal tinkle of glass.   powerpole

death puked me back out of its paunch: indigestible clump.   naked and suffering the return of sense

in a separate ward andy made no smash: wrack of lung.   scrap of chassis.   towed to the yard

what cried out in the woods between us.   the owl that shrieked: I was the one who shined into the ground

the ground refused me.   the ground that would leave the easy prey to be scavenged and take and take

[gary asleep in his recliner. this prison work clobbers him. today let the men stand unguarded]

gary asleep in his recliner.   this prison work clobbers him.   today let the men stand unguarded
he is overwhelmed by his own cells.   a furtive shiv behind his eyes: searchbeams opaque and anil

he dreams a wall: desert beyond where nothing is not jagged or barbed.   breathing hard he scales
hands numb nopales: swollen but withering inward nerveless.   the sensation of pinpricks

one long last watch: ectomorphic lockdown.   he draws the early pension.   incomplete his sentence

4

[nicholas the ridiculous: you will always be 27 and impossible. no more expectations]

nicholas the ridiculous: you will always be 27 and impossible.   no more expectations

you didn't carry those who went in long cars after you.   stacking lie upon lie as with children

swearing "no" to pain and "yes" to eternity.   you would have been a bastard: told the truth

afternoons I knelt beside your hiding place   [this is the part where you speak to me from beyond]

and he walks with me and he talks with me.   *he tells me that I am his own.*   dammit

nothing.   oh sure once in a while a dream.   a half-instant.   but you are no angel you are

repeating the same episodes: nick at night.   tricky nick.   nicholas at halloween a giant tampon

don't make me mature by myself: redundancy of losing common ground.   for once be serious

[kenny lost in *the mineshaft* among silver stalactites. his irises bloom in darkness]

kenny lost in *the mineshaft* among silver stalactites.　　his irises bloom in darkness

the night is an open "o."　　he caverns and groans engulfing:　largerbonessoulsweddingrings

leaking from the socket of his anus:　cocytus.　　he stands apart involuntary.　　pooped himself

false dreams it is often said take the entrance to this world for a home:　how he is led

of course nobody loves him.　　except the few who do.　　broad spaces of voicelessness

kenny crossing on the ferry.　　the ungenerous light of a moon hidden from view

he knows the way.　　he trembles bracing:　the hollow of his body delicately yields

[the thicknesses of victor decreased: blanket ⟶ sheet ⟶ floss. until no material would do]

the thicknesses of victor decreased: blanket ⟶ sheet ⟶ floss.   until no material would do

in the shedding season: the few of us who had not turned had found his remote room in mercy
he wriggled slight as a silkworm on its mulberry bed.   his lips spun slathering thread.   he sleaved

we waited for his release and he was released: yellow and radiant mariposa.   don't let us mend

[dead boys make the sweetest lovers. relationships unfold like stroke mags: tales less complex]

"...who could ever think—in particular, at this time, what gay man—that someone's death ever stopped the elaboration of someone else's fantasy about him?"

—D. A. Miller, *Bringing Out Barthes*

dead boys make the sweetest lovers.   relationships unfold like stroke mags: tales less complex

because they lack a certain tension.   several might be possessed and managed at once: properties

to be landed upon turn after turn: baltic ave.   st. james place.   time to roll those bones again

clean-cut jock in your treasure box: he is only ghost and polaroid.   your fist assumes his face:

the señor wences puppet trick.   his crack on the back so you can go both ways: brief resurrection

nudes prop themselves against the bed.   games evolve into storylines.   moments both pure and impure

the novel you write ends in many tragedies.   from which autobiography scarcely begins

8

[tall and thin and young and lovely the michael with kaposi's sarcoma goes walking]

tall and thin and young and lovely the michael with kaposi's sarcoma goes walking
and when he passes each one he passes goes "whisperwhisperwhisper."   star of beach blanket babylon

the sea washes his ankles with its white hair.   he sambas past the empty lifeguard tower
days like these who wouldn't swim at own risk: the horizon smiles like a karaoke drag queen
broad shoulders of surf shimmy forth as if to say "aw baby, sell it, sell it."   he's working again

towels lie farther apart.   the final stages: he can still do a dazzling turn but each day
smiles grow a little sharper.   he blames it on the bossanova.   he writes his own new arrangements

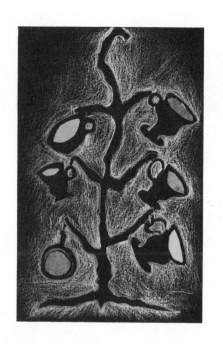

t e a   d a n c e

Eleven Disco Songs That Equate Sex and Death

Through an Elaborate Metaphor called "Heaven":

1. "Paradise" [Change]

2. "Heaven Must Be Missing an Angel" [Tavares]

3. "Angel Eyes" [Lime]

4. "Heaven Must Have Sent You" [Bonnie Pointer]

5. "Take Me to Heaven" [Sylvester]

6. "So Close to Heaven" [Trix]

7. "Be with You" [Sylvester]

8. "Tripping on the Moon" [Cerrone]

9. "Earth Can Be Just like Heaven" [The Weather Girls]

10. "Lift Off" [Patrick Cowley]

11. "Heaven's Where My Heart Is" [Marsha Raven]

—my personal "book of lists"

[heaven is a discotheque [*why don't you take me*] you could believe anything if you could believe]

heaven is a discotheque   [*why don't you take me*]   you could believe anything if you could believe

god is conveniently present when we need to shake our fists at someone.   strike the tambourine

because you are a comicstrip version of your earthly self: cussing in maladicta balloons:

exaggerated in posture/in glide/in blurgits.   even the clouds feel like getting lucky with you

let alone all those hermes.   yours for the plucking: *lining up from side to side on sunset*

you have strobed moments of elegance: sipping for example whatever kickapoo joy juice is there

"3 x's" brand perhaps.   haloed in the light from the billiard room.   you torture each panel

with your fine looks.   the possibilities puzzle you: deeper into the crosshatched corners

sundays go by same as ever: funnies and glittery tea dances.   you still don't get the punchline

[now the mirrored rooms seem comic. shattered light: I once entered the world through dryice fog]

"this was the season disco finally died"

—Kevin Killian, *Bedrooms Have Windows*

now the mirrored rooms seem comic.   shattered light: I once entered the world through dryice fog

not quite fabulous.   just young and dumb and full.   come let me show you a sweep of constellations:

16, I was anybody's.   favorite song: *dance into my life* [donna summer] and they did dance

17, first fake i.d.   I liked *walk away* [donna summer]   I ran with the big boys

18, by now I knew how to move.   on top of the speakers.   *give me a break* [vivien vee]

19, no one could touch me.   donna summer found god.   I didn't care.   *state of independence*

20, the year I went through the windshield.   sylvester sang *I want to be with you in heaven*

I said "you go" and "scared of you."   I listened to pamala stanley *I don't want to talk about it*

[the goodbye to nasty habits annual ball: scott smoking and drinking]

the goodbye to nasty habits annual ball: scott smoking and drinking

a new good riddance complete with that factory smell.   I wish them bluebirds

and o, how we danced on the night we divorced.   the ashtrays brimmed

bottles emptied into us: like thimbles to fill punch bowls.   and we sweated each other away

that was the morning of burnt out butts: dumpsters tall with those discarded abuses

the central nervous system cultivates a garden of tropisms about.   yes, it was a monday

who says that everything is explained in cycles.   work we once laid aside is taken up again

even the poorest taste has been developed: thirst defined by what quenches

a bad penny can be spent: on the useless.   or flattened by the weight of a moving train

to be taken out of circulation.   chain letter comes back unopened.   no: an invitation

[he'd make my bed jumble and squeak. a parrot must have lit inside. potty mouthed]

a song of Regan MacNeil

he'd make my bed jumble and squeak.   a parrot must have lit inside.   potty mouthed

I wouldn't have said, "quaquaquaquaqua" but his fingers pushed the dark: sores raised like letters

he wanted to gather all the air: buzzarding.   cold air flaps against the back of my skull

perched upon as a child bride: I felt my abdomen surge.   *captain howdy is kicking me*

hurt red pulp of a melon.   I bless the beak the tiny beak.   he has long black lashes like wings

[this is my last trick: if he has eyes they are escaping. the neighbors won't be able to describe]

a song of Sal Mineo

this is my last trick: if he has eyes they are escaping.   the neighbors won't be able to describe
when he flees his mane fans through the alley.   jerusalem palms beating against the doorway

in the blue hollywood hills behind the white hollywood sign where the falcons nest: I had lain
every letter shivered delighted under the swooping.   my feet drawn up into a careful vee

in the restroom at *the probe* I welcomed a sweet thrust.   pomegranate droplets dotted the commode

he was the disembodied voice of the planetarium.   I want to pretend it did not happen in the dark

[jackbooted. buttonflyed. hungering out of muni stations. spilling into clubs as sweet sweet tea]

a song of Patrick Cowley

jackbooted.   buttonflyed.   hungering out of muni stations.   spilling into clubs as sweet sweet tea
they chose me for a host: I was already carrying this choir in my head.   the language we share

the music had to magnify: silence would be unbear/unthinkable.   consider how sounds bodies make

now I lay me down these fierce tracks: bloodbeat & panting.   overtop an aspiration like release
music poured from me relentless.   no rest.   no rest.   a rapture bleating in the hills.   *going home*

joy for he whose song is done.   shirtless.   *before they say last call.*   I'm out among the multitude

[scott at arm's length: I hold him at mirror distance. his pelt is familiar is my own skin]

scott at arm's length: I hold him at mirror distance.   his pelt is familiar is my own skin

my fingers undo him.   I wonder what I'll look like inside his flesh.   tight as latex as thin

our hands gather at our middle: a corsage.   a leather coin pouch.   the zipper's poking tongue

he is almost colorless.   I have faded things that suit him.   his face is my face but young

ruts already deepening between us.   cannot stand to watch.   we both make fists of our eyes

when I leave he is discarded chrysalis.   what have I become: [change]   *I'll take you to paradise*

[and eventually I would take him back. into the reliquary of my mattress. winter terms]

and eventually I would take him back.   into the reliquary of my mattress.   winter terms

he stung like the briefest injection.   purples splotch inside the arms that were lifted by his grace

heaven can wait another hour for me.   I would use my teeth.   burn him with my whiskers

I spread him enormous and threadbare.   outside the world white as aspirin buries its hospital waste

my hands still clutch in an arc as large as his throat.   capillaries burst their deciduous branches

[between scott's asshole and his mouth I could not say which I preferred: perfect similes]

between scott's asshole and his mouth I could not say which I preferred: perfect similes
attention to cleanliness ran so deep.   I imagined a gleeming highway through the donner pass of him

a chill settling in his eyes: brown sierras.   I entered starving.   I could eat my weakest daughter

I want to hold a past larger than his shoes.   I want to say that summit closed its ribs around me
a story that omits resorts.   denies progress.   forgets how easily I traversed his altitudes

the truth: he was no monument.   sockets I plugged into.   warm circles I could make with my fingers
the truth: I have never left him.   I drive always toward california.   not all bodies are recovered

[fifteen and smooth. light petting for a first ten smackers earned. budget inn. a man from napa]

"when I was ten, thirteen, twenty—I wanted candy, five dollars, a ride."

—Essex Hemphill, *Ceremonies*

fifteen and smooth.   light petting for a first ten smackers earned.   budget inn.   a man from napa

we returned to the bar amid a dance of emergency lights.   one of many bodies I might have avoided

lips wrapped around his lifelessness: the swallow in mercy.   a throat unhinged to grouper size

[admission: I am a phag: afflicted with phagophagia]   seven times ruptured my esophagus:

1) betelnut. 2) greenglass. 3) pigbone. 4) spellingbook. 5) dressmakers' pins. 6) aspirin bottlecap. 7) comb.

and when I could afford to eat I ate away.   chewed hands off my ass.   chewed the saliva off tongues

[he must have been a deejay this one. the pulse quickens at another "lost companion" sale]

he must have been a deejay this one.   the pulse quickens at another "lost companion" sale

I filcher and dilber through crates of vinyl.   the glowing end of my glee cuffed in reverence

lovers carted away in stacks.   no needle to test them but I'm willing to take a chance

and the price is small.   any noise might easily be reduced: a matter of fading

the way the past is actively recaptured: not a whiff of poppers and halston z-14

no brief encounter with a surviving negative.   just a soundtrack undergoing reconstruction

he's a saint, he's a sinner [the mix as a product of survival]   pushing up to 144 bpm

[your shiny buckle unfastens at last. we who were always tarnished and dingged up had marveled]

your shiny buckle unfastens at last.   we who were always tarnished and dingged up had marveled
certain tim was only gotten with soft hands no teeth and the patience that never tears xmas wrap

what a handsome package you made: an after-meal brusher.   an "always says please and thank you"
always I knew your polish would fade.   good child gone bad: a talkshow loomed with you on it

I didn't have to be right.   look I am loving you as you aren't: be even that bright square again

s p i l l i n g   t e a

"And when they got back to the kitchen, the cooks and helpers would ask the servers,

'Well, did you spill the tea, girl?' Meaning, of course, was the gossip good?"

—Billie Gordon, *You've Had Worse Things in Your Mouth*

[how would ed lower himself to sleep with her. an elaborate rigging of wheels and piano wire]

how would ed lower himself to sleep with her.   an elaborate rigging of wheels and piano wire

butching up for the role: "tell the katzenjammers to amscray."   he'd banish her barnes

or he'd swagger her out to the supper club: the perfect beard.   cupping her hand on his arm

& bob might never have known.   no latent signs: ed ogling skirts.   mounding potatoes like breasts

he didn't come home late & stanky.   smelling of imitation passion [by lez taylor] & warm kootchie

yes bob understood infidelity: elevated it to a high art.   a social circle ripe with peccadillos

but the strings were known and pulled with masterful care: punch & punch.   punch & no judy

[she was not expecting another gentleman caller. a golden male had already been brought forth]

she was not expecting another gentleman caller.   a golden male had already been brought forth

knuckles squeezed around the silver bedrail: she tried to wish a daughter out her womb

I was unwelcome mercury boy: swaddled in fever.   kindled & cracked like firebrand in the hearth

snatched still blazing from the fever I was salvaged.   o the double almost waste of a pansied room

a little girl was thrifted out of what had been discarded.   no natural sonny grime beneath my nails

I could only work the gentlest garden rows.   playing sous-chef, yarn-winder, pin-cushion, maid

mothers enjoy their forgery.   now the passion has cooled for my malleable act: a girlchild fails

I bury her ash daily.   smudged fingerprints: smoothing the soft mound within me where she stayed

[piano strings severed. papa the only record of your passions has been this gift of abscissions]

piano strings severed.   papa the only record of your passions has been this gift of abscissions

now I know you once had a voice buttermilk sweet.   hands: a pendulous udder waiting to be stroked

[how I've glued you together: retrieved under the family mercantile one ledger mismarked "dairy"]

farmboys smirked when you sang at the nazarene church.   discreetly they sent you bovine kisses

your ivory ticklers faltered.   cheeks swollen in presentation: forceful bulls entered from behind

29

[untitled]

when did the darkness climb on with its muscular legs pinning me under: goodnight uncle boo

giant teeth grazed me: he descended from the clouds.   wanting to explore the downthere of me

the biggest thumb.   I had to go bathroom but vines held me fast.   beanstalk sprouting my pyjamas

at the foot of my trundle: magic beans could conjure him.   say it again: "I'll eat you up."

[a long line of bohunks and hunyaks: we settled in podunk. thirteen consonants]

a long line of bohunks and hunyaks: we settled in podunk.   thirteen consonants

surrounding a vowel with an umlaut.   that was the name we carried from ___tz___tz

into the new world.   in the grainbelt smackdab plopping down with our oxen and hogs

a cedar trunk in the junk-cluttered attic of a maiden aunt   [her name forgotten]

[so many ellipses in the tale of our begats]   keeper of tintypes.   christening gowns

the quilt patched out of hand-me-downs: scraps from grands and great-grands

difficult to say who we are in the present.   broadcast across farms like so many other seeds

threads of familiarity gradually unraveled.   whole generations apparently eaten by moths

[our family was tolerant of even anti-christs. but gramma had the recessive gene. now a lemon]

our family was tolerant of even anti-christs.   but gramma had the recessive gene.   now a lemon

the size of a lump grows in her bosom: she has bosom cancer.   *rock of ages cleft for me*

favoring jesus over her kith.   her kin ran away as soon as they mastered the knots of their laces

some never came home [remember uncle clyde's last photo: a sailor's arm draping him like foxfur]

we are sad to be burying her so late in life.   with our own wicked money: casting pearls

her 86 years would buy back four flames I had to shovel over.   were death but a swapmeet

go on to glory kind stranger.   with our first stumbling steps we followed the heathens next door

[mornings sagged and creaked in bed: from the coalpit of our too small sleep I always rose first]

mornings sagged and creaked in bed: from the coalpit of our too small sleep I always rose first

meteors had struck and cooled in the concavity between us.   each day I left him swathed and still

lukewarm scott curled on his side: repository of my abortions.   distant systole muted by a pillow

night our undoing.   I tugged at the knot of his navel: breech blue crater where the sky fell in

33

[my sister-in-law never uttered his name. solving the problem of the open field: house sprawl]

my sister-in-law never uttered his name.   solving the problem of the open field: house sprawl

landscape reinforces the oldest edict: go forth and multiply.   subdivide.   amortize

my sister-in-law sends me an article: "it's okay to be single."   I have always been to her

resisting options to buy.   legal documents.   floor plans.   nothing down on an enclosed space

bound as I could be to another man: meadow surrounded us.   we were made safe by distances

in-laws became a town unvisited.   now the ground is broken.   but barrenness still can last

[what happened to "significant" out of bed: abolished in the act of standing. like a "lap"]

"They were regularly gay. They were gay every day."

—Gertrude Stein, "Miss Furr and Miss Skeene"

your mom wanted you to get married.   she said.   and me standing right there.   her eye was fixing
beyond the shape of the neck you clung to at night.   we rubbed each other out: a pair of erasers

what happened to "significant" out of bed: abolished in the act of standing.   like a "lap"
otherwise we were only "others."   how significant could we remain even in vow

scenes from a wedding of two invisible men: roll after roll of over-developed film
all the world's mirrors won't have us.   at the cinemascopic margins: the eye must seek us

[who won't praise green. each minute to caress each minute blade of spring. green slice us open]

a song of mayflies

who won't praise green.   each minute to caress each minute blade of spring.   green slice us open
spew of willow crotch: we float upward a whirling chaff. sunlight sings in us *some glad morning*

when we are called we are called ephemera.   palpitating length of a psalm.   who isn't halfway gone
fatherless and childless: not a who will know us.   dazzled afternoon won't we widow ourselves away

t e a   r o o m s

"Even in the grocery store or the laundromat, every time someone's eyes passed over me, holding me for a second, I felt a boost that sent me forward and made me capable of doing anything."

—A. M. Homes, "The 'I' of It"

[what direction will you take when the universe collapses. you who when you go must go someplace]

what direction will you take when the universe collapses.   you who when you go must go someplace
you who must have more to spend than the rest of your life: busfare for instance.   mileage coupons

you have lived with yourself these several long years and wasn't that enough.   the awe now worn
behind the vacations of which you are fond: a flinch of terror.   your loins sag like a hammock

once men gobbled the garbo of you.   no wonder reclusiveness: in the russian river of your veins
the salmon are murmuring.   you go to your bungalow.   you know your bungalow dark as a birthmark

[this little kiddie liked floors: he'd go bangbangbang with his head all day long. hammerhead tyke]

this little kiddie liked floors: he'd go bangbangbang with his head all day long.   hammerhead tyke

he wanted to penetrate the world à la cartoon rabbit.   the world took its pokes: "why I oughtta . . ."

nevermind the needling: born and raised in the briarpatch.   chiggerspitbullsuncle: how he got dug

baby butt back with that thickboned brain of his.   enough force could put a place soft and round

noggin againstfloor againstbedpost againstwindshield.   against the day 'sgotta give and cut deep

[the last dog of this boyishness is put to sleep. feckless fluffy pet: I am not saved fella]

the last dog of this boyishness is put to sleep.   feckless fluffy pet: I am not saved fella

a bully tore me: he who muffled your bark with his shoe.   your sternum cracked the house unguarded

I stray for us both.   when the shelters are full I skulk among bins.   under fire escapes

spanked.   owned.   fed.   I have been all that: I wag the hanky in my backpocket receptively

boy my runty prayers are with you.   my legs kick at night automatic.   we chase the squeaky ball

better this way: run pant.   I have been his bitch.   you'd recognize the smell on me as killing

[the daddy purrs. he is holding a leopard speedo. tonight he takes his sugar to tea]

the daddy purrs.   he is holding a leopard speedo.   tonight he takes his sugar to tea
"precioçilla" the pinguid man calls me.   "put it on" he says & I put it on.   "take it off"

I take it and take this piddling attention.   my manners may be vile.   I may drink from the saucer

to be kept at all is eiderdown: scruffy denizen of the alley.   he took me in a bent brass lamp

when I am old I will vanish like a genie.   my master's wishes granted: boypussy, boypussy, boypussy
someday my knuckles big as his and split.   I'll try picturing what I'll have done with my hands

[my neck a toothsome feeding ground. vespered swarms had drunk of me before this new batman]

a song of Robin

don't be fooled by costumes: I am still an orphan.   I move through his house by stealth.   I thieve

he won't last: when he kisses I'll pull away.   already I know the short attention span of my body

my neck a toothsome feeding ground.   vespered swarms had drunk of me before this new batman

down every dark corridor of gotham I seek my next guardian.   capes fly open: how hunger rushes

when I'm ready to be circled one will circle.   secret cave.   I can make his voice bounce back

boy wonder.   he will believe he is the one hero.   I must remember to wince when I feel his fangs

[I wore the green bandanna as often as I could. cheaper than planefare. less baggage]

"When you see a pretty boy with the slave auctioneer, the assumption is that he wants to be sold."

—Catullus

I wore the green bandanna as often as I could.   cheaper than planefare.   less baggage

back when I was meat & potatoes and no fruit I scored: polk salad.   a wallet of greens

a common condition of chickenhood: legs replicate the shape of a brittle pull-y bone.   [snap!]

already accustomed to intrusion I worked.   muscles relaxed from age 3 as I recollect: preverbal

how such a trade is chosen: espaliered to bend.   to inhabit a particular corner

guess I wanted that avenue leading me away.   the same spot in my heart where traffic stopped

[these moves were not acquired overnight. stop: extended palm. love: suggestion of a hug]

these moves were not acquired overnight.   stop: extended palm.   love: suggestion of a hug

how many times did I learn to walk.   each new song an occasion of steps and turns

everyone saw that I was no ordinary canary.   talent scouts taloned me: chickenhawks

but mama said, "you can't hurry love, no"   what right did I have to assert these hips?

cheeks of putti blow me kisses from the cornice of a brownstone: partly the face is carved

and partly the wings insist.   I am not of this world.   I know others like me.   oh birdsong

[not even wanting to be the glamor puss: the chore in wardrobe. dressing an oversmoked voice]

a song of Julie London

not even wanting to be the glamor puss: the chore in wardrobe.   dressing an oversmoked voice

my sultry look wouldn't go 1 2 ways.   as in calendar girl.   as in a "girl can't help it" cameo

maybe I could reinvent the divorcee: the between-jack-and-bobby coquette.   slumming on la brea

if it could all be finale.   no jazz combo backing me into the limelight.   no rinse away hair

no burt reynolds luring me from retirement with plaintive air.   no cry me a fucking river

I could be happy in encino.   avoiding the reruns of me: nurse dixie mccall   [always "stat"]

fretting over a crossword I could have already done classic.   an excess of bubkes might please

[only the cruisy toilets will suffer this rascal. mmm, darlings. . . your smiles taste like porcelain]

only the cruisy toilets will suffer this rascal.   mmm, darlings . . . your smiles taste like porcelain

have I told you lately blahblahblah oh no?   pity.   but I hear the curfew knell & so must bid adieu

you alone would believe in the fictive heart: scarified as you are with that shape it's given

no permanent fixture the flesh.   remember a match skating in a urinal.   I escape like a gasp

your names are unsummonable.   extinguished cigs.   I reach toward your ceiling.   dangled man

[the city is dying to be stylish. if only it meant more ugly shoes: a return to eye contact]

the city is dying to be stylish.   if only it meant more ugly shoes: a return to eye contact

"girl be sensible" we want to say to fashion victims   [who become fashion vampires: no reflection]

they need to seem wan and bloodless.   trousers purchased sizes larger lend a pose of emaciation

in the windows of chichi stores dummies appear to be shrinking their waistlines: arriviste dummies

who's doing all this hair?   this lack of hair?   at the salon we flip through *oncology today*

some looks we look forward to looking back on.   remember ocean pacific.   remember angels' flights

[mannequins from the same lumber: correspondence of grains. perhaps the same grit finished us]

a song of Paul Cadmus's "Mannikins"

mannequins from the same lumber: correspondence of grains.   perhaps the same grit finished us

drawing us together.   sinistral hands overlapping the suggestion of genitalia.   we lack

no artist ever fills us in.   we sleep continent atop a history of unrequited pleasing

dumb showing.   we toy in earnest.   the attempt to conceal is also an attempt to divulge

[my stasis must confound you. if you have worshipped at all you must know what patience is required]

a song of Visconti's "Death in Venice"

my stasis must confound you.   if you have worshipped at all you must know what patience is required

see how the epicene tadzio trails behind the others: aware of your gaze and slightly bemused
you don't leave.   like that pitiful composer you're hooked.   yes you want to touch his hair

I must be fair now: the cobblestones are washed with bleach.   bedding smoulders in the piazza
irresistibility of endings: what if a flawless lad succumbs.   what if you catch your train on time

[rollingstock clatters through town and your cells urge to hop it. couplings of slatted cattlecars]

rollingstock clatters through town and your cells urge to hop it.   couplings of slatted cattlecars

the anatomy remembers where it came from: ~~####~~ .   shoulders hunch forward perpetually
the jab the belly anticipates.   out of habit eyes pull men in.   even the homely ones: Ⓧ

you could do a spread by rote.   [forgive the way the penis stirs at such a thought]
every inch of you courting [•].   rough and naff.   suppressing the gag response

a part of you will always pursue cars.   a suit of scars fitting to take that ride. ⚯

[not just that you and I got starry-eyed—an epidemic of romances was sweeping around us. a falling]

not just that you and I got starry-eyed—an epidemic of romances was sweeping around us.   a falling

in "love in the time of caulifleur" [documentary of that age] we're flanked by crowds of chemoheads
stalks of rappini towering in the public park: a sudden urgency grips each cruciferous vegetable

greensick in our salad days!   we cellophaned.   afraid of the rash our cravings would provoke
while the stench of toothy kisses wafted high.   in the streets we suspected passersby of sauerkraut

you were always firm to the touch: no signs of leafscorch or turnip blight.   rich in iron
and I picked at my plate: spat.   have the sidewalks wilted.   strike of the jealous sun

[elegy]

finally you are gone.   I began to think you the five brothers: each a different kind of indestructible

1) rugbaby, your mama hung you on the clothesline and worked you with a racket.   2) scalded you
3) were oopsed into a lake that spit you back.   4) intact your hard egg jigsawed a plate of glass

everyone [5) you included] took a crack.   you bounced back: ricochet biscuit?   *not this time, baby*
because the future cannot contain us: littleyou, littleme.   I drawing up the covers closed our eyes

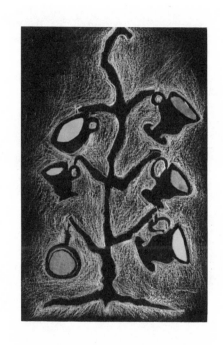

r e a d i n g   t e a

While on others thou art calling,

Do not pass me by

—Opening Hymn at Glide

[ode]

where have you gone blue middle of a decade?   the gates creak.   a sigh is so vastly different
the diary is pure spine.   in the most gingerly way each leaf opened reveals the less of you

83, 84, 85:   your relics in a converse box.   adoring letters from one upon whom you put the kibosh
shade trees bent to listen for a song.   [erasure?]   all of your best composing is lament

faithless time you steal the handsome petals for yourself.   a bruised fist of hyacinth becomes you
when the wind bears no whisper but alack: an eye fears you & distance: the short distance across

[the crash divides my life. before I hadn't been known to fly: the simon magus secret]

the crash divides my life.   before I hadn't been known to fly: the simon magus secret

I believe we shattered the same bone on impact: left humerus.   godbless us where the scars knit

a spot of earth still tastes of me.   where starthistles gorged themselves.   ittybites, bittybites

soft shoulders kiss in the slump of night.   I still wake with infant vision.   egypt wrapped

one prefers "accident" over "destiny."   I set out from the dyingplace.   these presents are my feet

hadn't I had them before?   my hair the color of mud.   indentations where my body chose to give

[divining: where I come from is drought. nine years at a time so arid we worry each drop. dread]

divining: where I come from is drought.   nine years at a time so arid we worry each drop.   dread

ten-year flood.   generations named before and after rain.   two kinds of cracks two kinds of damage

decade of evaporation: I remember children light as tumbleweeds.   some were carried by the wind

some sunk deep into wells.   when I drink I am thirsting for those springs: captives of hard earth

this year I'll not see the lake at its capacity.   scarcely the hope of a postcard: dam view

so full one cannot find where trees abbreviated.   tantalizing faces on the surface and below

[intolerable phoenix: the prairie. I come lately to an expanse unbroken by the human form]

intolerable phoenix: the prairie.   I come lately to an expanse unbroken by the human form

grasses clew a bestial sphere: foxtail and turkeyfoot.   seeding with the plangency of fire

where are my vacant young tenements now?   I thought the terror of memory was its inescapability

goldenrod grows where it always has.   up as if from subways: bright thatch continually streaming

I have no tie to unplotted land: transient milkweed.   flocculent discharge borne ever more aloft

[the merit of reading tea: gunpowder variety unfurls puptent green. sleeping bags zipped together]

the merit of reading tea: gunpowder variety unfurls puptent green.   sleeping bags zipped together

all summer our mouths wore the parfûm of shattered blossoms.   see: you like butter your chin says

in a clearing in the wood we were made to play nice & dainty: petite cookies amid elegant service

were we taught to rub two sticks together?   proper steeping.   poise and balancing upon the knee

our leaftips turn silver.   one would wander in search of cress: strangling in the creekbed

each discovery triggered by a broken cup.   using a trusty fieldguide to earn badges: we identify

[how his body stood against a thicket. rich in hardwood gentry: ponderous and gloomy]

how his body stood against a thicket.　　rich in hardwood gentry:　ponderous and gloomy
the limbs would still extend a noble canopy had they not been so alluring:　pitch and timber

hungry for plowland and pasture the notchers came.　　char and rot the tools for clearing
driven deep into tangles the aching teams.　　corduroy roads leading to the penetrable duff

he has been pioneered:　given to the final stump allowing settlement.　　slow collapse
these trees stripped and unable.　　there was no child in him:　a land traversed many times

signs dot the road where he should flourish.　　could the sparse line on a sign indicate the forest

[sleek mechanical dart: the syringe noses into the blue vein marking the target of me]

sleek mechanical dart: the syringe noses into the blue vein marking the target of me
haven't I always looked away.   don't want to see what's inside me.   inside me or coming out
older than balder: older than I'd planned to be.   aliveness jars me.   what's sticking what sticks

in my dream the haruspex examines my entrails.   glyphs of the ancient chitterlings transcribed:
highballs. speedballs. chirujos. chickens. lues. spora. blasphemy. butter. bitters. epicac.
highrisk behavior posterchild: come reeve.   a thousand happy tourists in-&-out me.   I matterhorn

how much frivolity does the hypodermic draw away: does it taste men waferthin who blest my tongue
does it know knees I've dandled on.   I feel taken in: darts in the waist of a coat I'll bury in

for I have husbanded recklessly: wedding daggers.   holes in my memory of holes: danaidic vessels
the needle quivers.   sickens.   I spill names an alphabetsoup of hemoglobin.   someone cracks the code

in a fortnight of waiting I draw up a will.   develop false symptoms.   how will I survive surviving

I'll throw parties where death blindfolded is spun: won't someone be stuck.   and won't I be missed

[my back is not straight. I have cradled the precious crutched and crutchless. crippled streets]

a song of Glide Memorial Methodist Church

my back is not straight.   I have cradled the precious crutched and crutchless.   crippled streets
the weight of these voyagers sways me.   I make strong jaws with my arms to hold them: lump of salt

wholecloth mouth unfolding.   the shout rattles along my roof.   eruption: a splintered pequod
my joy is leviathan.   in the bay the buoys are clanging.   I rise from the deep: gullet faithful

their gladness spills out on the land: I open wide a sextant.   let them find their bearings and walk on

64

[epithalamion]

say amen somebody.   the pews are hickory-hard I'm sick of sitting.   sick of hazy secondhand god

I'm gawky and greedy.   full of longing like frankie in "a member of the wedding."   here comes andy

alabaster betrothed: his pierced wooden groom casts a doleful glance.   *his eye is on the sparrow*

they took my heart gave thanks and brake it.   they are wounded by love: I must taste such a kiss

andy is lifted by outstretched arms.   slanted starlight and twisted shade.   I'm no more afraid

secretly I've brought my valise: "they are the we of me."   together we'll *steal away steal away*

[first fugue]

sweet birds sang: *there is trouble in paradise today.*   and we sweated each other away: shirtless

you and I afforded ourselves: a land traversed many times.   nights of undoing

lover divine and perfect comrade.   *I always wanted someone like you.*   now the ground is braking

visitation is brief but exact.   smiles grow a little sharper.   no more expectations

ears in lips and no more wit.   *and I'm still real hot then you kiss me there.*   we toy in earnest

slow tyranny of moonlight: dead boys make the sweetest lovers.   if they could all be   finale

they pass too quickly out of breath.   *I feel real when you touch me.*   the night is an open "o"

erased metropolis reassembled: the anatomy remembers where it came from.   up as if from subways

reveries are rivers: *why don't you take me to heaven?*   the shiny buckle unfastens   at last

3   "the owl that shrieked": from *Macbeth*.

4   "anil": indigo used as a bluing agent.

4   "nopales": young shoots of cactus.

5   "*and he walks with me* . . .": from the gospel song "In the Garden."

6   "*the mineshaft*": leather bar in New York (closed in the mid-1980s).

6   "cocytus": one of the four rivers of the underworld (in Virgil's *Aeneid*).

7   "mercy": hospital in Yuba City, California.

7   "sleaved": separated into filaments.

7   "mariposa": butterfly; also, in Mexico, a slang term for a queer man.

8   "señor wences": 1950s television personality whose ventriloquism act was performed with a puppet drawn on his fist.

8   "moments both pure and impure": from Tennessee Williams's *Memoirs*.

9   "*tall and* . . .": from the song "The Girl from Ipanema" by Antonio Carlos Jobim.

9   "beach blanket babylon": a campy stage show at Club Fugazzi in San Francisco.

13   "*why don't you take me*": from "Take Me to Heaven" by Sylvester. Sylvester died of AIDS in 1988.

13   "maladicta balloons": the indication, in cartooning, that a character is cursing.

13   "blurgits": also in cartooning, lines that indicate movement.

13   "*lining up from side to side* . . .": from "Sunset People" by Donna Summer.

13   "kickapoo joy juice": the name of Mammy Yokum's corn squeezings in the "Li'l Abner" comicstrip.

14   "donna summer": probably the only superstar of disco. She became a "born-again" Christian and spurned her queer audience.

14   "vivien vee," "pamala stanley": disco divas.

16   Regan MacNeil: the little girl in *The Exorcist* by William Peter Blatty.

16   "*captain howdy is...* ": from *The Exorcist.*

17   Sal Mineo: 1950s heartthrob, stabbed to death in 1974 by rough trade outside his apartment.

17   "in the blue . . .": see Robert Duncan's "My Mother Would be a Falconress."

17   "*the probe*": a bar in L.A.

18   Patrick Cowley: early pioneer of the "San Francisco sound" in disco. Cowley died of AIDS in 1982. The italicized segments are from Cowley's songs.

18   "sweet sweet tea": from Gertrude Stein's "Susie Asado."

20   "*heaven can wait . . .*": from "Tripping on the Moon" by Cerrone.

21   "donner pass": Interstate 80 from Reno to California, named after the ill-fated expedition who were trapped in the mountains during winter and who survived through cannibalism.

22   "phagophagia": a made-up word. I suppose it would mean "eating eating."

23   "filcher and dilber": the charwomen in Dickens's *A Christmas Carol* who steal the deceased Scrooge's meager possessions.

23   "poppers": amyl nitrate; once a popular inhalant both on the dancefloor and off.

23   "halston z-14": a popular fragrance in the early 1980s.

23   "*he's a saint . . .*": from "He's a Saint, He's a Sinner" by Miguel Brown.

23   "144 bpm": the beats per minute of a fast dance song.

27   "barnes": children (in Shakespeare's *Henry V*).

27   "lez taylor": a camp name derived from the former wifestyle of the rich and famous.

28   "firebrand": see Ovid's *Metamorphoses*, "The Brand of Meleager."

31   "bohunks and hunyaks": bygone ethnic slurs against folk of vaguely Eastern European descent.

32   "*rock of ages . . .* ": from the hymn "Rock of Ages."

33   "lukewarm": Scott's previous boyfriend was named Luke.

36   "*some glad morning*": from the spiritual "I'll Fly Away."

39 "garbo": reclusive star of yesteryear.

41 "hanky": the hanky code was a way of indicating various sexual impulses in the gay lexicon of the 1970s. A green hanky in the left rear pocket of one's trousers indicated that one was for sale.

42 "precioçilla": Spanish for "little precious one" (Gertrude Stein has a poem entitled "Precioçilla").

43 Robin: Batman's longtime companion.

44 "polk": a street in San Francisco once notorious for male prostitution.

45 "chickenhawks": in the queer lexicon, older men who like young boys—also known as trolls.

45 "putti": those happy angels on the sides of buildings.

45 "birdsong": Cindy Birdsong was the fourth Supreme.

46 Julie London: 1950s singer and actress. She was married to Jack Webb and then to jazz musician Bobby Troup, whom she met at a club on La Brea Boulevard.

46 "bubkes": a Yiddish word which means both "nothing" and "potato pancakes."

47 "a match skating . . . ": from *The Bridge* by Hart Crane.

48 "ocean pacific": a popular line of pseudo-beachwear (circa 1981).

48 "angels' flights": those polyester suits that made you look like you had no dick (of your own, anyway).

51 "rollingstock": a train.

51 ### : an inhospitable place (American hobo sign).

51 ⊗ : good for a handout.

51 ⊏·⊐ : danger.

51 ∞ : keep going.

51 "naff": "ugly"; allegedly short for "not available for fucking."

51 "do a spread": turn a trick.

52 "rappini": broccoli's Italian cousin.

53   "the five brothers": a story I remember reading when I was a child—five Chinese brothers who were identical and who each had a different superhuman power.

53   *"not this time, baby"*: from "This Time, Baby" by Jackie Moore.

57   "shade trees bent . . .": Ovid's *Metamorphoses*, "Orpheus and Euridice."

57   "erasure": also the name of a popular musical group of the 1980s.

57   "converse box": Converse was a brand of tennis shoes.

58   "simon magus": gnostic heretic who levitated and who was allegedly struck down by St. Peter.

60   "phoenix": the paragon of beauty. Also, the mythic bird that rose from its own ashes. Prairie grass must be burned back each season in order to reseed.

62   "corduroy roads": roads built of logs laid side to side.

62   "there was no child in him": from "A Woman Is Talking to Death" by Judy Grahn.

63   "balder": Norse god killed by a mistletoe dart.

63   "haruspex": seer who reads signs in the entrails of vivisected animals or humans.

63   "chirujos": in Mexican slang, queers.

63   "lues": syphilis.

65   "a member of the wedding": film version of Carson McCullers's eponymous novel. In the film, Ethel Waters sings "His Eye Is on the Sparrow."

65   *"steal away . . ."*: from the spiritual "Steal Away to Jesus."

67   [first fugue]: the lines begin with fragments from poems by William Shakespeare, Essex Hemphill, Walt Whitman, Paul Mariah, Frank O'Hara, Hart Crane, Robert Duncan, James Merrill and James Schuyler. The italicized lines are from Sylvester songs.

UNIVERSITY PRESS OF NEW ENGLAND publishes books under its own imprint and is the publisher for Brandeis University Press, Dartmouth College, Middlebury College Press, University of New Hampshire, Tufts University, and Wesleyan University Press.

ABOUT THE AUTHOR

D. A. Powell is a graduate of the Iowa Writers Workshop and is a recipient of a Paul Engle Fellowship from the James Michener Foundation. He lives in San Francisco.

LIBRARY OF CONGRESS CATALOGING-IN-PUBLICATION DATA

Powell, D. A.

Tea / by D. A. Powell.

     p.   cm. — (Wesleyan poetry)

ISBN 0–8195–6334–x (cl : alk. paper).

I. Title.   II. Series.

PS3566.O828T4   1998

811'.54—dc21   97–44599